Sitting Bull

Lisa Trumbauer
AR B.L.: 2.4
Points: 0.5   LG

Pebble™

First Biographies

Sitting Bull

by Lisa Trumbauer

Consulting Editor: Gail Saunders-Smith, Ph.D.
Consultant: Melodie Andrews, Ph.D.
Associate Professor, Early American History
Minnesota State University, Mankato, Minnesota

Capstone
press

Mankato, Minnesota

Pebble Books are published by Capstone Press
151 Good Counsel Drive, P.O. Box 669, Mankato, Minnesota 56002
www.capstonepress.com

1 2 3 4 5 6 09 08 07 06 05 04

Library of Congress Cataloging-in-Publication Data
Trumbauer, Lisa, 1963–
    Sitting Bull / by Lisa Trumbauer.
      p. cm.—(First biographies)
    Summary: Simple text and photographs introduce the life of Sitting Bull,
a Lakota chief who defended the American Indian way of life and traveled with
Buffalo Bill's Wild West Show.
    Includes bibliographical references and index.
    ISBN 0-7368-2371-9 (hardcover)
      1. Sitting Bull, 1834?–1890—Juvenile literature. 2. Dakota Indians—Kings and
rulers—Biography—Juvenile literature. 3. Hunkpapa Indians—Kings and rulers—
Biography—Juvenile literature. 4. Little Bighorn, Battle of the, Mont., 1876—Juvenile
literature. [1. Sitting Bull, 1834?–1890. 2. Dakota Indians—Biography. 3. Hunkpapa
Indian—Biography. 4. Indians of North America—Great Plains—Biography.
5. Kings, queens, rulers, etc.] I. Title. II. First biographies (Mankato, Minn.)
E99.D1S6238 2004
978.004'9752—dc21   2003011425

Note to Parents and Teachers

The First Biographies series supports national history standards for
units on people and culture. This book describes and illustrates the
life of Sitting Bull. The photographs support early readers in
understanding the text. This book also introduces early readers to
subject-specific vocabulary words, which are defined in the
Glossary. Early readers may need assistance to read some words
and to use the Table of Contents, Glossary, Read More, Internet
Sites, and Index/Word List sections of the book.

Table of Contents

Time Line

early 1830s
born

4

Sitting Bull

Sitting Bull was born in South Dakota in the early 1830s. South Dakota was not a state at that time.

area near where Sitting Bull was born

Time Line

early 1830s
born

Sitting Bull was a Lakota Indian. Lakota Indians hunted buffalo across the Midwest.

American Indian hunting a buffalo

Time Line

early 1830s
born

1857
becomes
war chief

Sitting Bull was a great leader. In 1857, he became the war chief of his tribe. He later became the tribe's chief.

Time Line

early 1830s
born

1857
becomes
war chief

Pioneers and Indians

Pioneers started moving west. They wanted to settle and farm in new areas of North America. Sitting Bull and other Indians lived in some of these areas.

Time Line

early 1830s
born

1857
becomes
war chief

Sitting Bull and other Indians believed in sharing the earth. But the pioneers did not want to share. They wanted to own the Indians' land.

Time Line

early 1830s
born

1857
becomes
war chief

1863
pioneers
look for gold

Fighting for Land

In 1863, pioneers moved to where Sitting Bull's tribe lived. The pioneers took their land and looked for gold. The United States ordered the Indians to move to reservations.

Time Line

early 1830s
born

1857
becomes
war chief

1863
pioneers
look for gold

The Lakota did not want to move. American soldiers fought Indians in the Battle of Little Bighorn. Many people were killed. The Indians won the battle, but they had to move anyway.

1876
the Battle of
Little Bighorn

Time Line

early 1830s
born

1857
becomes
war chief

1863
pioneers
look for gold

Later Years

Sitting Bull later traveled with Buffalo Bill's Wild West Show. Sitting Bull wanted to show people how Indians lived. He hoped this would help build peace.

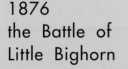
Sitting Bull (left) with Buffalo Bill

1876
the Battle of
Little Bighorn

1885
travels with
Wild West Show

Time Line

early 1830s
born

1857
becomes
war chief

1863
pioneers
look for gold

20

Sitting Bull was shot and killed in 1890 at his home. Today, people remember him for defending the American Indian way of life.

1876
the Battle of
Little Bighorn

1885
travels with
Wild West Show

1890
dies

Glossary

Battle of Little Bighorn—a battle in 1876 that Lakota Indians and other American Indians won against American soldiers; many Indians and American soldiers were killed in the battle, including the American leader George Custer; Sitting Bull did not fight in this battle.

Buffalo Bill—a famous buffalo hunter; Buffalo Bill had a traveling show about the Wild West; Buffalo Bill's real name was William Cody.

chief—the leader of a group of people

defend—to try to keep someone or something from being changed or harmed

Lakota Indians—American Indians who once lived mostly on the grassy plains of the Midwest

Midwest—the north-central part of the United States

pioneer—someone who moves to live in a new land

reservation—an area of land set aside by the U.S. government for American Indians

Read More

Aller, Susan Bivin. *Sitting Bull.* History Maker Bios. Minneapolis: Lerner, 2004.

McLeese, Don. *Sitting Bull.* Native American Legends. Vero Beach, Fla.: Rourke Publishing, 2003.

Silate, Jennifer. *Seeing the Future: The Final Vision of Sitting Bull.* Great Moments in American History. New York: Rosen Publishing Group, 2004.

Internet Sites

FactHound offers a safe, fun way to find Internet sites related to this book. All of the sites on FactHound have been researched by our staff.

Here's how:

1. Visit *www.facthound.com*

2. Type in this special code **0736823719** for age-appropriate sites. Or enter a search word related to this book for a more general search.

3. Click on the Fetch It button.

FactHound will fetch the best sites for you!

Index/Word List

Word Count: 217
Early-Intervention Level: 19

Editorial Credits
Mari C. Schuh, editor; Heather Kindseth, cover designer and illustrator;
    Enoch Peterson, production designer; Scott Thoms, photo researcher;
    Karen Risch, product planning editor

Photo Credits
Capstone Press, 10, 12, 14
Corbis/Bettmann, 4 (inset), 8; Tom Bean, 4
Getty Images/Hulton Archive, 1, 16, 18, 20
Library of Congress, cover
Stock Montage Inc., 6